Beautifully Broken

and the

31 Prayers

that Saved Me

By

Pameles D. Adams

Beautifully Broken and the 31 Prayers that Saved Me

ISBN: 978-0-578-88342-7

Published by Pamela Smalls Ball and SmallStories Publishing LLC.
Printed in the United States of America by Kindle Direct Publishing.

Hi... Come on in!

Congratulations on making the right choice! The next 31 days of your life will never be the same. My question to you is, "Will you keep doing what you are doing, or will you entrust the rest of your life to God?" Proverbs 16:9 (ESV) states, "**The heart of man plans his way, but the Lord establishes his steps**."

The chapters are short, but the prayers are deep and true. At the end of each prayer there is space for you to write your own personalized prayer or just a note to God. You can also list something that you are grateful for each day, and write a list of things you would like to continue to pray for or change in your life.

As you take this 31-day prayer walk, you may want to find a faithful and dedicated Christian friend, family member, co-worker, or spouse who will commit to being your accountability partner on this journey.

I pray that this book will show you that the power of prayer really works, that God loves you, and He has wonderful things in store for your life.

Table of Contents

Introduction

"I pray because I can't help myself. I pray because I'm helpless. I pray because the need flows out of me all the time, waking and sleeping. It doesn't change God. It changes me."

~ C.S. Lewis ~

The power of prayer is the greatest power of all. Sometimes we don't know how to pray, but we do know that prayer is our lifeline to God.

Why is it then that we find that it is so hard to find time to pray? We get distracted so easily with work, school, children, spouses, chores, friends, co-workers, social media, nightclubs…and the list goes on. You get the picture.

Before you beat yourself up about it, you have to understand that God doesn't seek our perfection; He longs for our presence. The Holy Spirit wants to teach us how to pray, and help us realize that prayer is not as complicated as we make it out to be. Maybe it's just me, but I feel that the enemy steps in when he knows we are about to speak with God.

The enemy will do whatever he can to distract us from praying, but whatever your challenges are in life, remember God is not looking for perfect words or perfect people. He just wants our hearts. So together, we'll look at how to pray when you are going through different situations.

Let's start now by saying a quick prayer.

God,

I pray right now for the one that is reading these words. I pray that if they are feeling weak, that You give them strength, I pray that if they are feeling broken, that You will put them back together again. God, if Your child is feeling lost, give them Your guidance. If they are feeling depressed, God give them Your grace. Help me to pray for others and let them pray for me.

In Jesus name I ask these things of You. Amen.

Prayer Reminders

1. *Prayer is simply having a conversation with God.*

2. *Prayer is not about the right words; it's about the right heart.*

3. *When you pray, believe that Jesus is enough for whatever you are facing.*

4. *Pray hardest when it is hardest to pray.*

5. *Pray for God's will to be done.*

6. *Pray through your pain, knowing God is with you.*

7. *Pray knowing that God is working even when you can't see His plan.*

8. *Pray boldly, knowing that God's timing is perfect.*

9. *Pray believing that in every place where you need a breakthrough, God is at work.*

10. *When you don't know where to start, the simplest yet most powerful prayer is one word – **JESUS**.*

The Lord's Prayer

The Lord's Prayer was one of the first prayers I learned as a child. The words come from Matthew 6:9-13 (KJV). There are many versions of the prayer but they all mean the same.

After this manner, therefore pray ye:

Our Father which art in heaven, Hallowed be thy name.

Thy kingdom come. Thy will be done in earth, as it is in heaven.

Give us this day our daily bread.

And forgive us our debts, as we forgive our debtors.

And lead us not into temptation, but deliver us from evil:

For thine is the kingdom, and the power, and the glory, forever.

Amen.

Just like we answer our emails each day, God answers our "Knee-Mail". The beginning of The Lord's Prayer, "Our Father which art in Heaven," is such a personal door-opener to God.

He is OUR father. He created you, loves you, and wants to hear from you! Daily!!!

Use the Lord's Prayer as a blueprint to communicate with God.

Your Personal Prayer

Word Search - The Lord's Prayer

M	S	A	L	S	E	F	O	R	G	I	V	E	N	G
U	F	A	T	H	E	R	L	L	L	W	I	V	Z	E
P	O	R	J	B	L	E	A	P	O	N	G	D	G	D
O	X	T	H	Y	W	I	L	L	R	K	A	P	L	A
W	I	O	I	L	D	E	H	R	Y	E	O	H	X	I
E	N	Z	H	V	A	G	D	H	T	A	M	E	N	L
R	G	T	F	A	T	H	E	T	X	R	L	A	C	Y
Y	E	X	I	D	L	W	B	R	H	T	R	V	E	B
G	U	V	U	N	N	L	T	A	C	H	V	E	M	R
D	E	L	I	V	E	R	O	E	H	L	O	N	W	E
E	O	L	Y	L	P	I	R	W	A	E	E	Z	R	A
B	L	S	E	G	N	O	S	H	E	A	S	L	F	D
T	N	A	T	A	L	K	I	N	G	D	O	M	O	M
S	D	R	M	A	D	E	P	H	O	P	S	X	N	I
S	T	E	M	P	T	A	T	I	O	N	I	N	G	E

Father	Thy Will	Earth
Hallowed	Debtors	Glory
Forgive	Temptation	Deliver
Lead	Amen	Evil
Power	Kingdom	Debts
Heaven	Daily Bread	

A Prayer for Anointing

"God gave you a gift of 86,400 seconds today. Have you used one to say

"Thank You"?

~ Dr. William Arthur Ward ~

Dear Heavenly Father,

Thank you for the man or woman reading this book. Anoint them and allow them to experience the power of prayer in these 31 days. Speak gently to them and affirm their hearts. Reveal Yourself to them in ways they could never imagine. May Your Holy Spirit lead them through each prayer, and inspire them to pray even more. May they mature into prayer warriors, for their families, their friends, their children, and anyone else who needs them.

Lord, if it is in Your will, renew them with grace and mercy. Help them to trust in You for all things, not some things. I pray a blessing over their hearts. God, ***Psalms 23:5 (NIV) says that You will prepare a***

table before them in the presence of their enemies, and anoint their heads with oil until their cup overflows. *Thank you Lord for the overflow!*

I also pray for protection over them. Please remove any temptation or evil from crossing the paths of your children. Bless this Man and Woman!

In Jesus' Name I pray, Amen.

Today I am Grateful for...

This is Day 1. Write down what it is that you are grateful for.

Date: _____ _____

Date: _____ _____

Date: _____ _____

Date: _____ _____

Date: _____ _____

Date: _____ _____

Date: _____ _____

Date: _____ _____

Your Personal Prayer

A Prayer for Stress

Dear Father God in Heaven,

I confess that I have let stress take a hold of my life, rather than give my burdens to You God. I have let stress come in and take control of my mood, my attitude, and my actions, and I'm falling apart with the pain and the stress of this game called LIFE. I am stressed, overwhelmed, tired, and totally confused, but I know that You are much greater than any problems that I have to face.

God, please be with me. You said in **Psalms 32:8 (NIV) that You will instruct me and teach me in the way that I should go, and that you will counsel me with your loving eye on me***.*

Please forgive me when my faith in You falls short. Father God, You are the Alpha and Omega, the beginning and the end.

God, please turn these possibilities for stress into lessons of growth and trust.

When I can't see any possible solutions, help me choose to believe that You are working things out for my good—in Your own time, as you have in the past.

In Jesus' Name I pray, Amen.

Today I am Grateful for...

This is Day 2. Write down what it is that you are grateful for.

Date: _____ _____

Date: _____ _____

Date: _____ _____

Date: _____ _____

Date: _____ _____

Date: _____ _____

Date: _____ _____

Date: _____ _____

Your Personal Prayer

_____

_____

_____

_____

_____

_____

_____

_____

_____

_____

_____

_____

_____

_____

_____

A Prayer for Strength

Dear God,

Thank You for all You have done in my life. You have showed up time and time again, and I believe You will show up now.

I feel like I've been running forever, trying to outrun this trial. Lord, I am not asking for You to take this trial away, for in **James 1:2 (NKJV) You said to count it all joy when I fall into various trials**. Instead, I am asking for the strength to endure this trial. I am asking You to help me stop outrunning my pain, and to give me the endurance to see this race to the end. I admit that life is hard, and sometimes I feel like I can't go on. I know that it is not Your intent to bring me this far and then leave me in this hard place alone.

Please God, give me the strength that I need to face today, and the faith that You will handle tomorrow.

In Jesus' Name I pray, Amen.

Today I am Grateful for...

This is Day 3. Write down what it is that you are grateful for.

Date: _____ _____

Date: _____ _____

Date: _____ _____

Date: _____ _____

Date: _____ _____

Date: _____ _____

Date: _____ _____

Date: _____ _____

Your Personal Prayer

A Prayer for a Troubled Marriage

Dear Heavenly Father,

My heart is in pieces knowing that some husbands and wives are ending what God has joined together. I pray that the Holy Spirit consumes the hearts of the men and women who are facing divorce.

I pray that You fill their spirits with peace and wisdom. May their love for each other be restored in Jesus' name. May they remember the reason they fell in love in the first place.

I pray for reconciliation and true forgiveness, God I know it is easier said than done, but may this experience be a part of their lives, so they can be a testimony to another hurting couple. Let their testimony glorify You God!

God, I pray against insecurity, depression, loneliness, and any other attacks that may come between these marriages. God, I pray for any shortcomings, or wrongdoings, that this man or this woman has done, be forgiven.

*Lord, I ask that like **Psalms 51:10 (NKJV) You create in them a clean heart and renew a steadfast spirit within them**. Release them from their past hurts.*

God, I ask that You help them to let go of the hurt, and rely solely on You for their healing.

In Jesus' Name I pray, Amen.

Today I am Grateful for...

This is Day 4. Write down what it is that you are grateful for.

Date: _____ _____

Date: _____ _____

Date: _____ _____

Date: _____ _____

Date: _____ _____

Date: _____ _____

Date: _____ _____

Date: _____ _____

Your Personal Prayer

_____

_____

_____

_____

_____

_____

_____

_____

_____

_____

_____

_____

_____

_____

_____

A Prayer of Thanks

Dear God,

Thank You! Because of what Your son, Jesus Christ, did for us, we are free from sin. We are covered by Grace and Mercy, and able to be righteous, because we are justified by the blood of Jesus Christ.

I thank You for everything that You have done in my life thus far. I am amazed when I think of Your everlasting goodness. Thank You Father for always watching over me, even when I couldn't watch over myself.

*God, I also thank You for protecting my children from dangers seen and unseen. God, You said in **1 Thessalonians 5:18 (NIV) to give thanks in ALL circumstances, because this is Your will for us in Christ Jesus**. Therefore, when this pandemic is over, I pray that each one of Your children has learned to lean, and depend, solely on You.*

God, I also thank You for those of Your children that are still working during this pandemic. God, I thank You for those that were able to receive unemployment benefits, as well as those that were able to receive food stamps, to be able to support their families. God, I thank You for the additional quality time they have to spend with their families, despite what they went through to get it.

And even though we are going thru this pandemic, I pray that we will experience consecutive wins, healing, unexpected blessings, financial freedom, and spiritual growth. I declare nothing about our lives will remain the same. No harm will come to us. No sickness will come near our homes. Lord, please command Your angels to protect us wherever we go.

In Jesus' Name I pray, Amen.

Today I am Grateful for...

This is Day 5. Write down what it is that you are grateful for.

Date: _____ _____

Date: _____ _____

Date: _____ _____

Date: _____ _____

Date: _____ _____

Date: _____ _____

Date: _____ _____

Date: _____ _____

Your Personal Prayer

_____

_____

_____

_____

_____

_____

_____

_____

_____

_____

_____

_____

_____

_____

_____

A Prayer for the Presence of the Lord

Heavenly Father,

You know everything that I am dealing with right now. I really need to feel the power of Your presence. I need to know You are here with me. Lord, help me to shift my focus away from my circumstances, and put it solely on You.

Thank You for exchanging my worries, frustration, and fear for Your peace. **Philippians 4:7 (NKJV) says that Your peace, which surpasses all understanding, will guard my heart and mind through Christ Jesus**. *Thank You for giving me Your peace, even when the circumstances are confusing. Help me to see things from Your perspective. Give me a glimpse of how You are working things out for my good.*

I choose to believe that no matter what happens today, tomorrow, or next week, You will give me the Grace and Mercy I need to overcome it all.

Thank You for being my joy and my strength, and for helping me to be a dispenser of Your hope for those around me today. Lord, help me to forever remember what a gift it is to sit with You like this.

In Jesus' Name I pray, Amen.

Today I am Grateful for...

This is Day 6. Write down what it is that you are grateful for.

Date: _____ _____

Date: _____ _____

Date: _____ _____

Date: _____ _____

Date: _____ _____

Date: _____ _____

Date: _____ _____

Date: _____ _____

Your Personal Prayer

_____

_____

_____

_____

_____

_____

_____

_____

_____

_____

_____

_____

_____

_____

_____

_____

A Prayer for Hardship

Lord,

HELP ME!!! While I am going through this hardship, help me cling to your promises. I know the only way I will be able to face these difficulties is by placing my trust in You. You give me strength. You give me understanding. You give me guidance. Thank You Lord! Please lead me and grant me victory over my hardships.

God, please let there be good news in my life and in my home. **Psalms 111:2 (NKJV) says the works of the Lord are great**, and I am confident that I am going to win this fight, because it is You who started this great work in me.

I thank You for Your divine light and grace, given to me every day. I may not be worthy, and I may not be pure or perfect, but I beg You to be merciful. For with Your grace and favor, I go on to improve each day.

In Jesus' Name I pray, Amen.

Today I am Grateful for...

This is Day 7. Write down what it is that you are grateful for.

Date: _____ _____

Date: _____ _____

Date: _____ _____

Date: _____ _____

Date: _____ _____

Date: _____ _____

Date: _____ _____

Your Personal Prayer

_____

_____

_____

_____

_____

_____

_____

_____

_____

_____

_____

_____

_____

_____

_____

A Prayer for YOU

Dear Father God,

Thank You for the work You are doing in my life. I am so grateful for every breath that You allow me to take. I am grateful for every new opportunity that You bless me with each and every day.

I am so grateful for Your Grace and Mercy. It is so amazing! I know that the plans You have for my life cannot always be seen by me.

*You said in **Jeremiah 29:11 (NIV) that You know the plans You have for me…plans to prosper me and not to harm me…plans to give me hope and a future**, and I believe that if I hold steadfast, Your plans will surely be revealed to me one day.*

Thank You for giving me air to breathe. Thank You for surrounding me with favor. Everything is not perfect, but I know You are on the throne. I am grateful to be alive. I am grateful for my family and friends. I am grateful for the opportunities that You have blessed me with.

I know that You are the Alpha and Omega, the beginning and the end! I know Your promises are true, so I place all my hope in You. I promise not to seek approval or validation from the world, but I will seek it from Heaven above.

God, I pray that You continue to give me peace and understanding and most of all...wisdom. Let Your will and promises always be a meditation of my heart.

In Jesus' Name I pray, Amen.

Today I am Grateful for...

This is Day 8. Write down what it is that you are grateful for.

Date: _____ _____

Date: _____ _____

Date: _____ _____

Date: _____ _____

Date: _____ _____

Date: _____ _____

Date: _____ _____

Date: _____ _____

Your Personal Prayer

_____

_____

_____

_____

_____

_____

_____

_____

_____

_____

_____

_____

_____

_____

_____

A Prayer for My Family

Dear Holy and Almighty Lord,

I ask You right now to please protect my family from any harm, misfortune and sadness. Increase their faith, and protect them from falling into temptation. Please keep the enemy at bay.

Father, I ask that You bless our times spent together. Let it be filled with blessings and memories. Allow us to experience joy, celebrate happy occasions, and be there for each other. Let us respect, and listen to one another. Begin with me, dear Lord, and let the change first happen in me.

*Allow me to be like the woman You spoke of in **Proverbs 31:15 (NIV), who gets up while it is still night, and provides food for her family**. Show me how to love more. Show me how to care more. Show me how to listen more. Show me how to forgive. Show me how to be more compassionate.*

Let Your spirit change in me, so my family will know that if You did it for me, You can also do it for them.

In Jesus' Name I pray, Amen.

Today I am Grateful for...

This is Day 9. Write down what it is that you are grateful for.

Date: _____ _____

Date: _____ _____

Date: _____ _____

Date: _____ _____

Date: _____ _____

Date: _____ _____

Date: _____ _____

Date: _____ _____

Your Personal Prayer

A Prayer to Thank YOU

Dear Father God,

Thank You for Your grace that allows me to be able to recognize this new day as a new chance to walk closer with You.

Thank You for today. Thank You for this hour. Thank You for this minute. Thank You for this second. Thank You God! Thank You for waking me up this morning in my right mind. Lord, just as in **Psalms 118:21 (NIV) I will give You thanks, for You answered me, and You have become my salvation.**

God, please continue to be a hedge of protection around me and my family. God, please remove anyone in my life who was not sent by You, or anyone sent to cause me harm. Thank You for loving me, right where I am, just as I am.

In Jesus' Name I pray, Amen.

Today I am Grateful for...

This is Day 10. Write down what it is that you are grateful for.

Date: _____ _____

Date: _____ _____

Date: _____ _____

Date: _____ _____

Date: _____ _____

Date: _____ _____

Date: _____ _____

Date: _____ _____

Your Personal Prayer

_____

_____

_____

_____

_____

_____

_____

_____

_____

_____

_____

_____

_____

_____

_____

_____

A Prayer for My Sins

Dear Heavenly Father,

I come to You as humbly as I know how. I come to confess my sins, those known and unknown. For in your word, **1 John 1 (KJV) says if I confess my sins, You are faithful and just to forgive me my sins, and to cleanse me from all unrighteousness***.*

Lord, You know that I am not perfect, and I fall short each and every day of my life, but I want to take time out to say thank You, Thank You for new mercies that You bestow upon me each and every day.

I reflect on the many ways I have failed to do the right thing by You. I accept that I have made many mistakes. I have lied, cheated, gossiped, been dishonest, and lusted. I was angry at other's good fortunes. I've coveted the things of others. I've flirted and played with temptation. I pray that You help me to deal with the emotions I'm experiencing as a result of my mistakes.

Please lead me, sustain me, and help me heal from the pain and shame that I am going through. Father, please help me to remember that I am a child of God, and give me the power to make it through this season, and all the seasons to come.

In Jesus' Name I pray, Amen.

Today I am Grateful for...

This is Day 11. Write down what it is that you are grateful for.

Date: _____ _____

Date: _____ _____

Date: _____ _____

Date: _____ _____

Date: _____ _____

Date: _____ _____

Date: _____ _____

Date: _____ _____

Your Personal Prayer

A Prayer of Thankfulness

Dear Holy and Almighty Lord,

I am so grateful for Your word in my life. God, thank You for all the guidance that You have provided to me. Thank You for all the times You kept me out of darkness, and showed me the light, and for the times You kept me in the darkness, because I was not ready to see the light. **1 Thessalonians 5:18 (NKJV) says in everything give thanks; for this is the will of God in Christ Jesus for me,** *and for that, I am truly thankful.*

I am so grateful that I can turn to You in good times, and in times when it feels like I can't go on. God, thank You for always hearing my cry. Thank You for protecting me when I am faced with painful situations. Thank You for Your great love and care. Thank You for Your sacrifice so that I might have freedom and life.

In Jesus' Name I pray, Amen.

Today I am Grateful for...

This is Day 12. Write down what it is that you are grateful for.

Date: _____ _____

Date: _____ _____

Date: _____ _____

Date: _____ _____

Date: _____ _____

Date: _____ _____

Date: _____ _____

Date: _____ _____

Your Personal Prayer

_____

_____

_____

_____

_____

_____

_____

_____

_____

_____

_____

_____

_____

_____

_____

_____

_____

A Prayer to change My Heart

Dear Father,

Please help me. Give me a strong amount of love, patience, and understanding for others, no matter what my circumstances may be.

*Please give me the strength to love again, for **1 John 8 (NIV) says whoever does not love does not know God, because God is love**. Help me to not see fault in anyone, because You see no fault in me. Help me to remember that no one is perfect.*

I am overwhelmed, distraught, and exhausted. I am not sure how to let You carry my heavy load, but I know only You can. Please Lord, take it from me. Let me rest and be refreshed, so that my heart won't be so heavy in the days to come.

I am confident that You will work wonders on my behalf. I'm asking You to fight for me, and bring me through to victory. God, You are so amazing, and powerful. Thank You for my many blessings.

In Jesus' Name I pray, Amen.

Today I am Grateful for...

This is Day 13. Write down what it is that you are grateful for.

Date: _____ _____

Date: _____ _____

Date: _____ _____

Date: _____ _____

Date: _____ _____

Date: _____ _____

Date: _____ _____

Date: _____ _____

Your Personal Prayer

_____

_____

_____

_____

_____

_____

_____

_____

_____

_____

_____

_____

_____

_____

_____

_____

_____

A Prayer to cover My Children

Dear Heavenly Father,

Praying to You is the biggest weapon that I have to protect and raise up godly children. For years, I've used scriptures, and prayed for my children in all circumstances, good and bad, known and unknown.

I've prayed for their strength, compassion, kindness, wisdom, love and understanding, patience and protection. ***Hebrews 4:12 (NIV) tells me that the word of God is alive and active. It is sharper than any double-edged sword, cutting between soul and spirit, joints and marrow. It judges the thoughts and attitudes of the heart.*** *This means Your word lives and breathes through me!*

Cover my children daily Lord. I pray for their covering many times throughout each day. I ask that You ***put the full armor of God on them, so that they can stand against the devil's schemes and plots like you promised in Ephesians 6:11 (NIV).***

Father God, I invite you into my home and ask for Your anointing spirit to rest upon my children. As I send them out into the world, I pray their feet are equipped with the readiness of peace, the belt of truth, firmly worn, with the breastplate of righteousness to help them do the right thing in Your eyes. Father, I ask for my children to be firmly protected in their armor with the shield of faith. Help my children ward off the enemy's flaming arrows, and give them faith in the unseen, which is You.

Lord, I pray for a hedge of protection around my children as they engage in the world today. Let Your presence guide them, and Your warrior angels fight for them.

In Jesus' Name I pray, Amen.

Today I am Grateful for...

This is Day 14. Write down what it is that you are grateful for.

Date: _____ _____

Date: _____ _____

Date: _____ _____

Date: _____ _____

Date: _____ _____

Date: _____ _____

Date: _____ _____

Date: _____ _____

Your Personal Prayer

_____

_____

_____

_____

_____

_____

_____

_____

_____

_____

_____

_____

_____

_____

A Prayer to start My Morning

Dear Almighty God,

I thank You that my name was on the wake-up list this morning. Lord, I pray that nothing separates me from You today, tomorrow, or ever.

You said in **Psalms 118:24 (KJV) that this is the day which You hath made, and I shall rejoice and be glad in it.**

Today is a new day. A chance for a new start.

Yesterday is gone, and with it any regrets, mistakes, or failures I may have experienced.

Help me to walk according to the Word, and not my feelings.

Help me to keep my heart pure and undivided.

Protect me from my own careless thoughts, words, and actions.

Keep me from being distracted by MY wants, MY desires, and MY thoughts on how things should be.

Help me to embrace what comes my way as an opportunity, and not a personal inconvenience.

*You said in **Psalms 86:13 (NIV) that great is Your love toward me.***

You already know that I will fall short and mess up from time to time, but God, give me the faith to know that You will get me back in line.

In Jesus' Name I pray, Amen.

Today I am Grateful for...

This is Day 15. Write down what it is that you are grateful for.

Date: _____ _____

Date: _____ _____

Date: _____ _____

Date: _____ _____

Date: _____ _____

Date: _____ _____

Date: _____ _____

Date: _____ _____

Your Personal Prayer

_____

_____

_____

_____

_____

_____

_____

_____

_____

_____

_____

_____

_____

_____

_____

A Prayer for the Armor of God

Dear Heavenly Father,

Today, this second, I claim victory over the enemy, because **Ephesian 6:11 (NKJV) says if I put on the whole armor of God, I will be able to stand against the wiles of the devil***.*

I have on my belt of Truth, standing on Your truth alone.

I have on the breastplate of Righteousness, remembering that I am clothed in the righteousness of Christ.

I have on my shoes of Peace, for today, and all the days to follow, I will walk in Your peace.

I thank You for the Helmet of Salvation, which lets me know that I am Yours, and that no one or nothing can ever take me from Your hands.

In Jesus' Name I pray, Amen.

Today I am Grateful for...

This is Day 16. Write down what it is that you are grateful for.

Date: _____ _____

Date: _____ _____

Date: _____ _____

Date: _____ _____

Date: _____ _____

Date: _____ _____

Date: _____ _____

Date: _____ _____

Your Personal Prayer

_____

_____

_____

_____

_____

_____

_____

_____

_____

_____

_____

_____

_____

_____

_____

_____

_____

A Prayer when it's Hard to Pray

Dear God,

In life, difficult times will definitely come, if they haven't already. But I know that I have to just keep living or P.U.S.H. (Pray Until Something Happens).

My faith has been tested, over and over again, but I know that I should never let my problems define who I am. Prayer changes my situation every time!

I have many questions in my heart. Why me? Why now? I have prayed to you God. I have fasted and studied the word. I have received revelation, but nothing in my life has changed yet.

Heavenly Father, I don't understand what is going on in my life right now. It's too hard to keep pushing. You are big enough to change it. You are loving enough to want to, yet nothing seems to change in my eyes.

But God, I want a change. I need a change. I don't like where I am. I don't want this. I am crying out to You for help. I want Your will to be done in my life. My way of handling things is not working. I want to surrender!

Lord, help me to let go of what I think is good, and trust in You. God this is hard. Lord help me through! Help me to accept what is, let go of what was, and have faith in what will be. God You know what You are doing.

*Lord, You said in **II Chronicles 7:14 (NKJV) that if Your people who are called by Your name will humble themselves, and pray and seek Your face, and turn from their wicked ways, then You will hear from heaven, and will forgive their sin and heal their land**. Heal my land Lord! Heal me!*

In Jesus' Name I pray, Amen.

Today I am Grateful for...

This is Day 17. Write down what it is that you are grateful for.

Date: _____ _____

Date: _____ _____

Date: _____ _____

Date: _____ _____

Date: _____ _____

Date: _____ _____

Date: _____ _____

Date: _____ _____

Your Personal Prayer

_____

_____

_____

_____

_____

_____

_____

_____

_____

_____

_____

_____

_____

_____

_____

A Prayer to follow God Today

Dear Heavenly Father

When I pray to You God, I always want You to answer my prayers instantly.

I believe in the power of prayer, but when it comes to my life and my problems, I often don't have the faith to believe God will answer my prayers, because sometimes it takes so long, but I know that God's timing is always on time.

Lord, today is Your day, and I want Your will to be done. So, whatever happens, hold my hand and let's face it together.

*You told me in **Deuteronomy 6:14 (NIV) not to follow other gods, or the gods of the peoples around me**. So, I will continue to follow You Lord!*

I don't know who or what will cross my path today, but I do know that I am going to follow Your word today God.

Help me to walk by faith and not by sight. Help me to believe in Your truth and not my feelings. Help me to embrace anything that comes my way today, because I know that I have You by my side and nothing can happen to me.

In Jesus' Name I pray, Amen.

Today I am Grateful for...

This is Day 18. Write down what it is that you are grateful for.

Date: _____ _____

Date: _____ _____

Date: _____ _____

Date: _____ _____

Date: _____ _____

Date: _____ _____

Date: _____ _____

Date: _____ _____

Your Personal Prayer

_____

_____

_____

_____

_____

_____

_____

_____

_____

_____

_____

_____

_____

_____

A Prayer for God's Promises

Dear Gracious Father,

Please forgive me for I have been so wishy-washy when it comes to taking hold of Your promises and making them mine. But today, I'm putting my foot down! I will not allow my human problems to talk me out of my spiritual inheritance from You.

God, please be with me. You said in **2 Corinthians 12:9-10 (NIV) that Your grace is sufficient for me, for Your power is made perfect in weakness. Therefore I will boast all the more gladly about my weaknesses, so that Christ's power may rest on me**.

God, Your promises to me are always YES and AMEN, and your promises are for me 24/7, 365 days a year. God You are so merciful, faithful and gracious toward me.

Lord, You **promised** to work all things together for the good of those who love You.

*You **promised** to prepare an eternal home for me in heaven, where sin, sickness, and sorrow don't exist.*

*You **promised** to fight for me.*

*You **promised** to forgive me and cleanse me from unrighteousness, if I confess my sins to You.*

*You **promised** to supply me with wisdom, if I only ask.*

*You **promised** to know me intimately.*

*You **promised** to never grow weary.*

In Hebrews 13:8 (NIV) You said that Jesus Christ Is the same yesterday, today, and forever. *May I live each day of my life in the power of Your promises!*

In Jesus' Name I pray, Amen.

Today I am Grateful for...

This is Day 19. Write down what it is that you are grateful for.

Date: _____ _____

Date: _____ _____

Date: _____ _____

Date: _____ _____

Date: _____ _____

Date: _____ _____

Date: _____ _____

Date: _____ _____

Your Personal Prayer

A Prayer to love My Life

Dear God,

As I reflect over the last three years of my life, I am reminded of Your grace, love, mercy, and favor. My soul feels like it is broken into a million plus pieces.

I have so many concerns and cares, and they weigh me down often. But it's still my life. Each and every day I wake up and I put on a smile to cover up the hurt and the pain.

God, show me the good things that I often overlook. Help me to be content with what I have, and to stop complaining about what I don't have.

Please forgive me when I compare myself, and my situation, to others. I need to go through my tests so that I can turn them into testimonies. Thank You for loving me right where I am, and just as I am.

God, help me to love the life that I am living right now. **Proverbs 18:21 (NKJV) says that death and life are in the power of the tongue, and those who love it will eat its fruit**. *I want to be fruitful Lord!*

Forgive me for longing for things outside of You and Your kingdom. Help me to keep my eyes on You.

In Jesus' Name I pray, Amen.

Today I am Grateful for...

This is Day 20. Write down what it is that you are grateful for.

Date: _____ _____

Date: _____ _____

Date: _____ _____

Date: _____ _____

Date: _____ _____

Date: _____ _____

Date: _____ _____

Date: _____ _____

Your Personal Prayer

_____

_____

_____

_____

_____

_____

_____

_____

_____

_____

_____

_____

_____

_____

_____

A Prayer to Bless My Job

Dear Father,

Thank you for all the ways You've blessed me, specifically with this wonderful job that pays my bills, and puts food on my table. Help me to view my work as a blessing and not a curse. Give me grace and strength to stay focused on my job.

When I am tempted to give up, and want to quit, help me to keep going. Grant me a cheerful spirit when things don't go my way. Help me to control my attitude.

Allow me to be as the virtuous woman you spoke of in **Proverbs 31:17-18 (MSG), so that first thing in the morning, I can dress for work, roll up my sleeves, and be eager to get started! Let me sense the worth of my work, and be in no hurry to call it quits for the day.**

Lord, please help me to not be quick to anger, or to get upset when my day at work is not going so great. Help me to do all that my job has called me to do. Help me to see my co-workers as you see them.

Finally, Lord, give me the patience to see my work day through from beginning to end.

In Jesus' Name I pray, Amen.

Today I am Grateful for...

This is Day 21. Write down what it is that you are grateful for.

Date: _____ _____

Date: _____ _____

Date: _____ _____

Date: _____ _____

Date: _____ _____

Date: _____ _____

Date: _____ _____

Date: _____ _____

Your Personal Prayer

A Prayer before I Sleep

Dear Almighty God,

*As I prepare myself to lay down tonight, I ask that You dispatch Your loving angels to watch over me as I sleep. You said in **Proverbs 3:24 (NIV) that when I lie down, I will not be afraid, and that when I lie down, my sleep will be sweet**.*

I ask that You relax the tension in my body, calm the racing of my mind, and still the thoughts which worry and perplex me.

God, please allow Your spirit to speak to my heart while I am asleep, so that when I wake up in the morning, I will have a clean heart.

*God, I ask that You forgive all my sins from today, and grant me a good night's rest, so that tomorrow, I can experience a brand-new day. For as You said in **Psalms 4:8 (NIV) in peace, I will lie down and sleep, for You alone, Lord, make me dwell in safety.***

In Jesus' Name I pray, Amen.

Today I am Grateful for...

This is Day 22. Write down what it is that you are grateful for.

Date: _____ _____

Date: _____ _____

Date: _____ _____

Date: _____ _____

Date: _____ _____

Date: _____ _____

Date: _____ _____

Date: _____ _____

Your Personal Prayer

_____

_____

_____

_____

_____

_____

_____

_____

_____

_____

_____

_____

_____

_____

_____

_____

_____

A Prayer when you're having a Rough Day

Dear God,

Reset my life please! Today has been, by far, the roughest day I have had in a while. Everything that could have possibly gone wrong has went wrong.

I overslept this morning.

I couldn't find the right outfit to wear.

I didn't have time to get coffee.

My car was giving me trouble.

I have no gas in my car.

All of these obstacles in my way caused me to arrive to work late!

Father, please guide my heart. Allow me to feel it beating and know that I am still alive, and that I have a purpose!

Yes, I had a rough day today, and I will have more rough days in the future, but I will never give up, as long as You are by my side!

For you told me in **Matthew 6:34 (NIV) not to worry about tomorrow, for tomorrow will worry about itself, and that each day has enough trouble of its own**.

So, I will stand on Your word, and trust in You Lord for all my tomorrows.

In Jesus' Name I pray, Amen.

Today I am Grateful for...

This is Day 23. Write down what it is that you are grateful for.

Date: _____ _____

Date: _____ _____

Date: _____ _____

Date: _____ _____

Date: _____ _____

Date: _____ _____

Date: _____ _____

Date: _____ _____

Your Personal Prayer

_____

_____

_____

_____

_____

_____

_____

_____

_____

_____

_____

_____

_____

_____

_____

A Prayer when you're Seeking Answers

Dear Heavenly Father,

I am so ashamed of myself at times. Sometimes, I sit and ask myself why did God create me? Why am I the way that I am? Am I not enough? Am I not pretty enough? Am I not smart enough? What is it Lord?

Sometimes the answers come right away, and sometimes, I have to wait on Your timing. For I know that your answers may be delayed, but never denied.

You said in **Matthew 7:7-8 (NIV) that I can ask and it will be given to me; if I seek, I will find, and if I knock, the door will be opened for me. For if I ask, I will receive, if I seek, I will find, and if I knock, the door will be opened**.

Thank You for answering all my prayers in Your perfect timing with Your perfect answer, even though I may not always understand Your answer.

In Jesus' Name I pray, Amen.

Today I am Grateful for...

This is Day 24. Write down what it is that you are grateful for.

Date: _____ _____

Date: _____ _____

Date: _____ _____

Date: _____ _____

Date: _____ _____

Date: _____ _____

Date: _____ _____

Date: _____ _____

Your Personal Prayer

A Prayer when life gives you Lemons

Dear God,

I have had many sour experiences in my life. Someone that I consider to be close to me has hurt me.

Lord, please help me to make lemonade from these lemons. I have some lemons in my life that I feel like I will never recover from. I battle with self-doubt, and low self-esteem.

I have been dealt a bad hand at times. Help me to play the hand that I have been dealt, and meet my obstacles head on. One by one, Lord, I want to give them to You.

Lord, You said in **James 1:2 (NKJV) to count it all joy when I fall into various trials, knowing that the testing of my faith produces patience**. I want You to grant me the patience Lord, to understand that my trials are here to make me strong!

Thank you for continuously blessing me, just as You do every day. These lemons can make my attitude sour at times.

Help me to remember that when life throws me lemons, I can call on Jesus to help me make the sweetest lemonade.

In Jesus' Name I pray, Amen.

Today I am Grateful for...

This is Day 25. Write down what it is that you are grateful for.

Date: _____ _____

Date: _____ _____

Date: _____ _____

Date: _____ _____

Date: _____ _____

Date: _____ _____

Date: _____ _____

Date: _____ _____

Your Personal Prayer

_____

_____

_____

_____

_____

_____

_____

_____

_____

_____

_____

_____

_____

_____

_____

A Prayer for my Finances

Dear God,

I know that I am not the only person on this planet who is stressed about money. Day after day, month after month, I lose sleep over how I am going to pay my bills.

My money is so tight right now. Groceries, rent, utilities, car payments, insurance, gas, and clothing all have to be paid. Sometimes I wonder if I will ever stop living paycheck to paycheck.

*God, I am praying for a financial blessing for me! God, I surrender all my financial concerns to You, for You said in **Psalms 77:14 (NIV) that You are the God who performs miracles, and You display your power among the peoples.***

God, as I look at my finances, I realize that I have more bills than I have money, so right now, God, I ask that You look down on my home with pity, and send me relief in a way that only You can.

*You said in **Ephesians 3:20 (NIV) that You are able to do exceedingly abundantly above all that I ask or think**, and I stand on Your financial promise to me.*

*I find myself boldly repeating these three words daily: **God will provide.** Provide for me Lord!*

In Jesus' Name I pray, Amen.

Today I am Grateful for...

This is Day 26. Write down what it is that you are grateful for.

Date: _____ _____

Date: _____ _____

Date: _____ _____

Date: _____ _____

Date: _____ _____

Date: _____ _____

Date: _____ _____

Date: _____ _____

Your Personal Prayer

_____

_____

_____

_____

_____

_____

_____

_____

_____

_____

_____

_____

_____

_____

_____

A Prayer for Peace

Dear Loving God,

Please grant me peace in my mind, body, soul and spirit. I ask that You heal and remove everything that is causing stress, grief, and sorrow in my life.

I surrender, and admit that I cannot control people, plans, or even my circumstances, but I can yield those things to you, and focus on my peace, for You said in **Isaiah 26:3 (NKJV) that You will keep me in perfect peace because my mind is stayed on You, and because I trust in You**.

Thank you today for every good gift You've given, every blessing You've sent, all the forgiveness I did not deserve, and for every trial You've allowed into my life. I joyfully receive your peace.

In Jesus' Name I pray, Amen.

Today I am Grateful for...

This is Day 27. Write down what it is that you are grateful for.

Date: _____ _____

Date: _____ _____

Date: _____ _____

Date: _____ _____

Date: _____ _____

Date: _____ _____

Date: _____ _____

Date: _____ _____

Your Personal Prayer

_____

_____

_____

_____

_____

_____

_____

_____

_____

_____

_____

_____

_____

_____

_____

_____

A Prayer of Gratefulness

Dear Father,

Thank you for allowing me to awaken to yet another beautiful day. I am grateful for the beauty of the sun, and Your other creations. I first have to tell You that I am so grateful for the gift of life.

I want to take a minute, not to ask for anything from You, but to simply share my gratitude to You. Just like in **Psalms 107:1 (NKJV) I give thanks to You, for You are good, and Your mercy endures forever***! Thank you Lord!*

I am so grateful for Your unfailing love towards me. I am blessed beyond measure.

You said that You will never leave me, nor forsake me. You are always with me. I am so grateful for what I have, and therefore, I will not complain about what I don't have. I am so grateful for Your amazing power!

I love You and I need You Lord, today and every day. I give You all my praise and thanks, for You alone are worthy! Because of You, I am more than a conqueror through Christ who strengthens me!

In Jesus' Name I pray, Amen.

Today I am Grateful for...

This is Day 28. Write down what it is that you are grateful for.

Date: _____ _____

Date: _____ _____

Date: _____ _____

Date: _____ _____

Date: _____ _____

Date: _____ _____

Date: _____ _____

Date: _____ _____

Your Personal Prayer

_____

_____

_____

_____

_____

_____

_____

_____

_____

_____

_____

_____

_____

_____

_____

A Prayer for Encouragement

Dear Lord,

I am a firm believer in encouraging others. You are always encouraging and uplifting me to find my true purpose and peace in You.

Life happens fast! One day, things are fine, and the next day, things seem to hit me out of left field. One day, everything is fine, and then the next, I get kicked down.

God, You said in **Philippians 4:13 (NKJV) I can do all things through Christ who strengthens me.** So Lord, encourage the Holy Spirit that lives inside of me. Motivate me to know that I can do it! Give me a daily supply of strength to endure the tests each day.

Lord, please encourage me! Encourage my sister and brother today. Lord, You said in **Psalms 118:24 (NKJV) this is the day that You have made, and I will rejoice and be glad in it**!

Lord, as you encourage me, let me be an encouragement to all those around me.

Help me to keep getting up.

Help me to keep following You.

Help me to stay on Course.

Help me to keep hoping, and holding on to the joy and peace Jesus died to give to me. He is my ultimate source of encouragement.

In Jesus' Name I pray, Amen.

Today I am Grateful for...

This is Day 29. Write down what it is that you are grateful for.

Date: _____ _____

Date: _____ _____

Date: _____ _____

Date: _____ _____

Date: _____ _____

Date: _____ _____

Date: _____ _____

Date: _____ _____

Your Personal Prayer

A Prayer to Be Saved

Dear Heavenly Father,

For a long time, I have tried to keep You out of my life, thinking I could do life on my own. I know that I am a sinner and that I cannot save myself, so I come to You today to confess my sins, and to ask for Your forgiveness.

You said in **Romans 10:9 (NKJV) that if I confess with my mouth the Lord Jesus and believe in my heart that God has raised Him from the dead, I will be saved.** *So, I come to You today, to confess my sins, and to humble myself unto you.*

Come into my heart as my Lord and Savior. Create in me a clean heart. Take complete control of my life, and help me to walk in Your footsteps daily, by the power of the Holy Spirit.

I am grateful that You have promised to keep me, despite my many sins and failures. Thank You for hearing my prayer.

In Jesus' Name I pray, Amen.

Today I am Grateful for...

This is Day 30. Write down what it is that you are grateful for.

Date: _____ _____

Date: _____ _____

Date: _____ _____

Date: _____ _____

Date: _____ _____

Date: _____ _____

Date: _____ _____

Date: _____ _____

Your Personal Prayer

A Prayer to just Be You

Dear Heavenly Father,

There are times in my life that I think I need to question You, and ask why my life is the way that it is? I know that I am not the only one. But You said in **Job 42:4 (NKJV) for me to listen, and let You speak, and that You will question me, and I will answer You**.

I feel like I am supposed to be further along than I am. Every time I take three steps forward, here comes the curve ball that throws me five steps back.

But I thank You, because the one thing You keep telling me is, "Never be who you're not." You always tell me to be myself, bravely and unapologetically.

So moving forward, each day, I will strive to Be motivated. Be encouraging. Be forgiving. Be beautiful. Be open. Be loving. Be humble. Be thoughtful. Be unstoppable. Be knowledgeable. JUST BE ME!

In Jesus' Name I pray, Amen.

Today I am Grateful for...

This is Day 31. Write down what it is that you are grateful for.

Date: _____ _____

Date: _____ _____

Date: _____ _____

Date: _____ _____

Date: _____ _____

Date: _____ _____

Date: _____ _____

Date: _____ _____

Your Personal Prayer

_____

_____

_____

_____

_____

_____

_____

_____

_____

_____

_____

_____

_____

_____

_____

_____

The Serenity Prayer

God, give me grace to accept with serenity

the things that cannot be changed,

Courage to change the things

which should not be changed,

and the Wisdom to distinguish

the one from the other.

Living one day at a time,

Enjoying one moment at a time,

Accepting hardship as a pathway to peace,

Taking, as Jesus did,

This sinful world as it is,

Not as I would have it,

Trusting that You will make all things right,

If I surrender to Your will,

So that I may be reasonably happy in this life,

And supremely happy with You forever in the next.

Amen.

Conclusion

Well, here we are at the end of our journey. I was Beautifully Broken, and these were the 31 prayers that saved me!

I end this devotional by reminding you that God is not looking for perfect people with perfect words, but He is looking at the intentions of your heart.

I'll never be perfect, but I love that I am welcome into the presence of God just as I am. If you are living your life without God, and without prayer, your life will become toxic. Not having Prayer in your life will cause you to have a negative spirit, and keep you from believing that anything new is possible for you.

Even at the bottom, there are certain things you can control, and certain things you cannot. For everyone trying to control the outcome of their lives, God wants to set you free from thinking you know what He needs to do for you. It will overwhelm you trying to figure out God's plan for your life.

The best thing you can do with the losses, the loss of hope, the loss of family members, the loss of faith, the loss of energy, the loss of relationships, the loss of hardship, is to humbly bring them all to God.

We have One who is always with us, who always has time for us, who will never leave us. God cares about everything going on in our lives, big or small.

On the days, weeks, and months, when God seems to be silent, and nothing is making sense, just know that He is still working on your behalf, even though you don't understand His plans for you.

I'm excited to see what God has in store for you and me, as we move forward together. Remember, He is the God of the impossible!

My Ultimate Thanks

To God, the One and the Almighty,

This has been a journey, a long road, and a long time coming for me. I'm thankful that You have given me the gift to write and inspire others. Sharing my life stories will impact others in ways that I cannot even imagine.

Thank You, God! Thank You, Father! Thank You, Lord!

Thank you for creating me to be a living vessel and an inspiration to others. Thank you for allowing me to survive my tests and tribulations, and for allowing me to share my testimony to help someone else overcome their tests.

Amen!

Special Thanks

To all of my supporters...thank you all so much for believing in me when I sometimes didn't believe in myself. Some have come and went, but the faithful few remained loyal in spite of the trials, tests, or outcome of situations throughout my life. I thank you all for remaining in my life, because that's something that has been very rare in my life. You all always came through and made me feel so special.

I would like to thank you for taking this life journey with me. I love you today, tomorrow, and forever; butttt....

The best thanks goes out to Author Pamela Smalls Ball. This lady has been everything to me and more. Words really can't express how I feel about her, so I have to try and sum it up. Pamela took my words that I had on a regular piece of paper, and turned them into magic. She turned them into a finished product that I thought I would never finish. I am grateful for her vision, her hand, her creativity, and her patience with me. Pamela, I thank you so much! I am forever grateful to you.

From the Author

A lot of Blessings have come my way lately. Why? Because I began to think positively, and let go of all the negative things and people that were weighing my spirit down, and holding me back. God will remove certain things and people out of your life that meant you harm, and will replace them with the people you need, and the people who really care about you.

Let's set the record straight…I'm just a nobody, trying to tell everybody something good. I am often unsure of myself at times, and I struggle with confidence issues. Why do I share this? Because I had to change a lot of things in my life, starting with myself, and if I can do it, you can too.

I know that the only reason I am here today is because God spared my life. I've made a lot of mistakes in my life, and I'm not talking about one or two mistakes either. I've even stooped to the level of some who were immature, and not deserving of my time and energy.

I had to stop and check myself. I've pushed people away who truly cared about me, and that hurts. I had to change my circle, my mentality, and my attitude from negative to positive. I had to go to God, and ask him to heal my heart and soul. That's when my Blessings started to come.

Many of you don't know this, but if it wasn't for all the continued support, prayers, midnight talks, and getting cursed out, I probably would not have followed through with publishing my second book. Putting my writing out there the first time was scary. It still is! But I want to say, thank you to those of you who read my first book and asked for more.

Thank you to those who continued to encourage me throughout the entire publishing process. Thank you to everyone who recommended "The Hand I Was Dealt" to their friends, and continued to spread the word about this new author. Thank you to everyone who showed up for my first book signing to show your support. Thank you to everyone who reviewed my book. There is no greater gift to an author than a positive review.

Most importantly, I would like to give a big thank you to both sets of parents, who have always been there for me, my three beautiful children, my friends, and every single one of you who have supported me from day one. You've inspired me to continue to go after my dreams. You've brightened my darkest days, and you've helped me to believe that I can do anything I set my mind to, and change what I once thought was impossible to possible! For that, I will forever be grateful to you.

I'm telling you all of this from experience. God will work miracles in your life when you improve yourself. I'm not perfect, and I don't know anyone who is. I still have a lot of work to do on myself, but I am determined to stay on a positive path with God.

Now that I have finished writing my second book, I am still in disbelief that in August of 2019, I published my first book! I keep saying to myself that this is not real! But it is! I am on the front cover of a book! I am on Amazon! With God's Grace and Mercy, I am! Thank you!

In Memory of my Grandmother
Mary B. Perry

To my beloved grandmother in Heaven Mary B. Perry. I Love you even in death. You passed away two days before my birthday back in 2009, and I now understand why. God needed you more, and now you are my guardian angel. It was you who kept the family together like glue (super glue), and you are the reason why I am the woman I am today...a phenomenal woman.

Your house was my favorite place to be when I was a little girl, and you were the one I always enjoyed talking to the most, to get that good old wisdom from back in the 60's and 70's. My heart smiles at the thought of our conversations and our Bingo nights together. We had our date nights at least three nights a week. No one will really understand Bingo the way that I do.

Grandma I will always love you and will always make you proud of me. I pray that you continue to watch over me, until I see you again.

Love, your Granddaughter

About the Author

Pameles D. Adams, is the only child of Diane Walls, Bobby Howze Jr, and Robert Walls. Her inspiration to write and speak to the world came from her life's journey. Her passion is to share knowledge, wisdom, love, and bring hope, motivation and inspiration to all.

She loves to share her story of how God met her when she was at her lowest point, and lifted her up again. To new life and a New Beginning!

Her message: GOD IS FOR YOU!!

Pameles has been through a lot in her life, has courageously overcome difficult challenges, and discovered ways to help others.

Now Pameles is an Author, Certified Life Coach, and Motivational Speaker, who combines her wisdom and skills to services others.

Most importantly, she is a child of God, a mother of three, and a grandmother.

Pameles is dedicated to giving, and reminding people that they must change their mindset and their inner talk, in order to change their lives.

Pameles believes that with self-inventory, hard work, and perseverance, anything is possible. She has not yet discovered all the answers in life, but she is willing to learn as she grows.

Remember YOU CAN LIVE THE LIFE YOU'VE IMAGINED!

Pameles loves God and a Good cup of coffee.

Father, I ask you to make ready for this reader to tell the people why they believe. Father I ask that you make way for my reader to accept what is, let go of what was, and always have faith in what will be, because you always know what you are doing.

Dear Father God,

I come to you in the precious name of Jesus Christ asking you to HELP my reader forgive and release every negative thing that has made them cry, to feel alone, to feel that they are not enough, over the years and to replace that with happiness, laughter, love Grace and Mercy.

Father I pray that this devotional and prayers blesses them as they continue on this journey called LIFE.

In Jesus' Name I pray, Amen.

www.ingramcontent.com/pod-product-compliance
Lightning Source LLC
Chambersburg PA
CBHW081151090426

42736CB00017B/3265